CW01654112

The 21 Day
Go for No!®
Challenge

Richard Fenton
& Andrea Waltz

This Workbook Belongs to:

Published by

SUCCESS IN 100 PAGES
SHORT BOOKS. BIG IDEAS.

www.SuccessIn100Pages.com

ISBN 978-1-947814-69-1

LEGAL DISCLAIMER:

Every effort was made to ensure the accuracy of the information within this book was correct at time of publication. The authors and publisher do not assume, and hereby disclaim, any liability to any party for any loss, damage, or disruption caused by errors or omissions, whether such errors or omissions result from accident, negligence, or any other cause. If you apply the ideas contained in the book, you are taking full responsibility for your actions, and there is no guarantee you will duplicate the results stated here. Every individual's success is determined by his/her desire, effort, knowledge, and motivation.

It has been said that the word 'NO' has destroyed more lives than all the wars since the dawn of time.

We believe this to be true.

But it doesn't have to be that way—at least, not for you.

-Richard Fenton & Andrea Waltz

"It's funny. Even when I intentionally aim for the 'NO' basket, some of my planes accidently end up in the 'YES' basket. If I keep this up long enough, the 'YES' basket will fill up all on its own."

Welcome to the 21 Day Go for No!® Challenge

Introduction

Dear High Performer:

Welcome to ***The 21 Day Go for No!® Challenge,*** a program designed to help you start the process of reprogramming how you think about failure and rejection by intentionally increasing your failure rate for a specific period of time.

How Does the Challenge Work?

In some ways, it works any way you want it to—after all, it's *your* challenge! But this doesn't mean there's no structure. We've created a series of steps to get ready along with a process by which you challenge yourself to get a certain number of NOs in a defined period of time.

And we're going to presume that makes sense to you. Because we'll assume you read the book, *Go for No! Yes is the Destination No Is How You Get There,* or maybe you've heard us speak at an event or on a podcast. In any case, hopefully you have a basic understanding for what Go for No! is all about. (The 21 Day Go for No! Challenge workbook is <u>not</u> intended as a replacement for reading our book and, ideally, taking our full Go for No! Online Course.

By the way, this is not merely an attempt to get you to buy more of our training—it's to give you the greatest chances at changing your thoughts, behaviors, and to get the results you want from your job, career, and your life.)

That said, this guide will not teach you the fundamentals of the concept itself or train you in a specific aspect of it. Instead this challenge is all about putting the Go for No! ideas into action to get results.

Dale Carnegie said:

> *"Inaction breeds doubt and fear. Action breeds confidence and courage. If you want to conquer fear, do not sit home and think about it. Go out and get busy."*

That's our goal for you during the next 21 days—to go out, get busy, and collect as many NOs as you can, knowing that in the process the yeses you're looking for will happen in greater quantities than you expect.

A Little Background…

After writing the book, we spent three years creating an in-depth training program called *Mastering Go for No!*®, comprised a series of core concepts—from strategies on how to use Go for No! as well as the mindset needed to do it. (Note: the new and improved online version is now available at **GoforNoCourse.com**).

As part of that initial program, we encouraged people to do the Go for No! Challenge to ensure they put what they'd learned into practice.

And the best part about a challenge is anyone can do it—from telemarketing sales, door to door, B2B, B2C, retail, for whatever product, service, or sector all the way to actors auditioning for roles and writers submitting their book proposals. If you can *go for no,* you can do a Go for No! challenge.

Over the years, thousands of people have done their own challenges with great success. We realized we'd been hiding a really important tool for helping people apply the concepts and this workbook was born.

We are excited that you've made the decision to do this.

It's amazing what can happen in just a few weeks when you challenge your assumptions and your self-imposed limitations.

Benefits of the Challenge

The main benefits of doing this challenge include:

#1: To Grow Sales.

This challenge is designed to increase the opportunities to bring in revenue. That means prospecting, as well as expanding the size of every sale or upselling. And asking for referrals. Someone has to offer something and the outcome—a yes or a no—gets measured. We want to impact those numbers.

That said, in doing so you will also stop just focusing on people who you have somehow predicted will say yes to you. It's the true essence of what it means to Go for No!

#2: To Plant Seeds.

This challenge is designed to keep you from being depressed after getting a no and slowing down your momentum and talking yourself out of achieving your goals.

When you go for no you keep going and stay focused on your sales activities, planting the seeds necessary for future business to come your way. Because the reality is, you might not reap the benefits of this challenge immediately. But you will in the future.

And then you will want to do challenges every quarter just to take advantage of the momentum it can create!

#3: To Reduce Stress.

This challenge is designed to reduce your fears and stress when it comes to hearing no. The more you hear it, the more it will lose its power over you. That's how you build confidence. And then guess what? You have more fun. By the way, when you are having fun, selling is far easier. People are attracted to it.

Ever met an unhappy, stressed salesperson? It's a silly question because, of course you have. Did you buy more or less? Or at all? If you did have to buy, it wasn't pleasant was it? Not the way to build a great business.

#4: To Expand Your Comfort Zone.

Finally, the Go for No! Challenge is designed to help you expand your current comfort zone. And, yes, you do have a comfort zone that limits your performance, whether you think you do or not. We all do.

The comfort zone is a combination of patterns we're comfortable with—patterns and routines that are the brain's way of helping us minimize stress, reduce risk, and create a state of mental and physical security. Unfortunately, the consequence of reducing stress and risk is that we also reduce opportunities for growth, development, and reward.

The Go for No! Challenge is designed to challenge you outside your comfort zone for a short period of time, to experience what you could be achieving.

Use Go for No!® the Right Way

Few people dream about being a salesperson when they were ten years old: astronaut, cowboy, firefighter, yes—movie star, ballerina, baseball player, absolutely—but sales? No, probably not. This isn't because there's anything intrinsically wrong with selling, it's just not as glamourous or exciting as other things. As such, we didn't ask for sales training for Christmas, and you've probably never had a kid show up at your door at Halloween dressed as a used car salesman.

The largest profession in the world just happens to be selling, and one of the highest paid, too. Sadly, it also ranks consistently among the ten most hated. The ironic part is that the world needs salespeople more than virtually any other profession.

So why has a profession so important and highly paid as sales developed such a bad reputation? It's because of negative experiences with pushy salespeople who lied, tricked and/or pressured you and sold you something you didn't want. That's it. There's no other reason. Even most salespeople hate salespeople.

The truth is, no one hates salespeople—they hate self-centered, highly-manipulative, fast-talking, stereotypical "snake oil" salespeople who care only about making the sale and not about them.

Conversely, people love and appreciate good salespeople who help them buy products and services that change their lives for the better. They appreciate them so much that they go back and buy from them over and over again.

The key to overcoming the negative internal stigma you may be carrying about being in sales is to shift from being a self-centered "salesperson" to a customer-centered "sales consultant" who operates with the prospect's interest in mind while simultaneously pursuing the objective of making the sale.

Is this possible? Is it possible to be customer-centric and be a top performing salesperson? Yes, assuming you do it with the proper selling style.

The Four Selling Styles

There are two primary concerns that drive most sales behavior. They are:

- **RESULTS** (making the sale and generating profit/income)
- **RELATIONSHIPS** (customer satisfaction with the process)

When you cross-reference these two concerns, from Low to High, there are four very distinct "selling styles" that emerge:

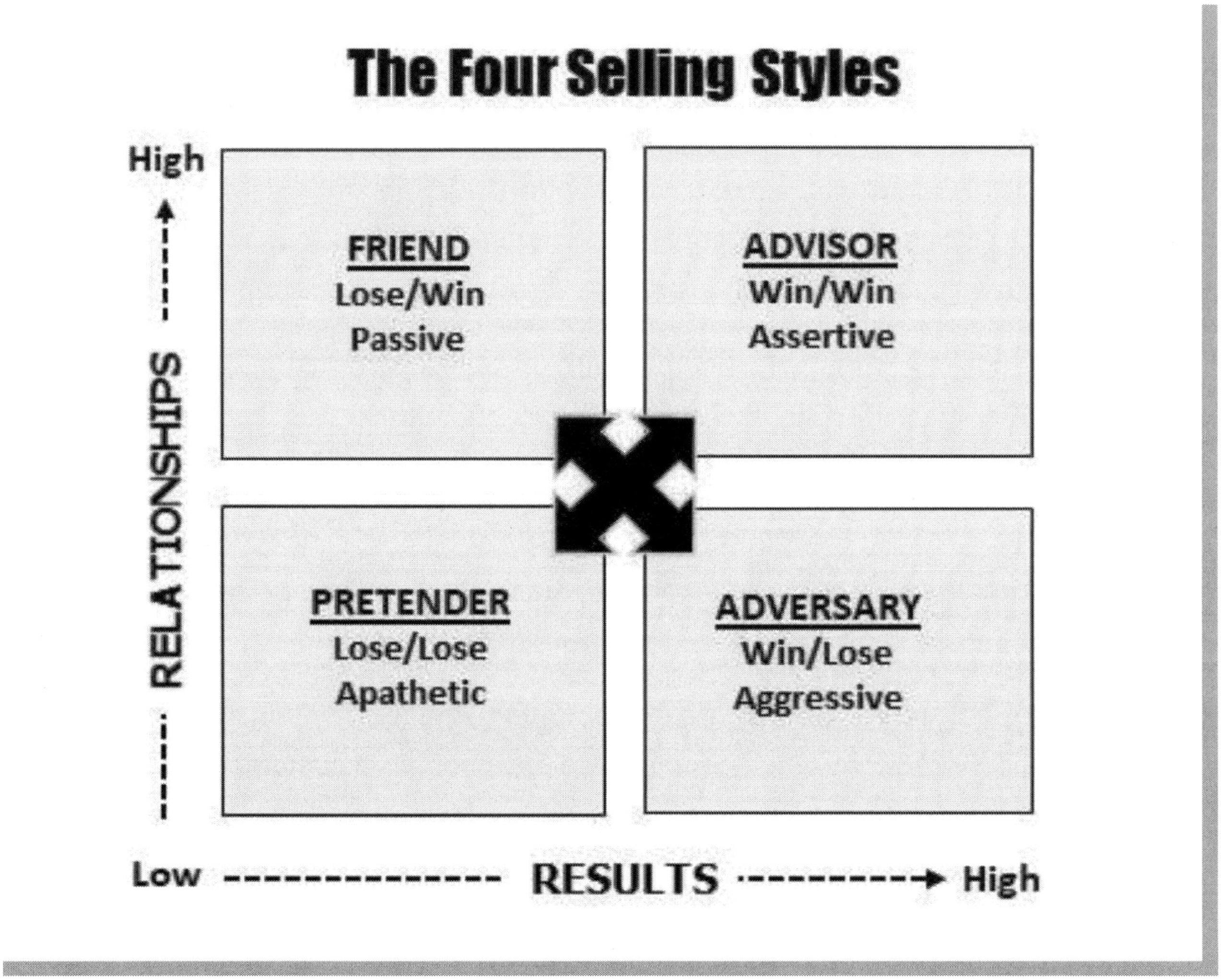

Let's look at each, one at a time:

Selling Style #1 (lower right)

THE ADVERSARY

While we wish it weren't true, there are actually salespeople who go into every interaction with the attitude that what is taking place is a battle—a *war of wills* in which either they or the prospect will emerge victorious. Their goal is to "WIN" the sale, even if it means that the customer must LOSE in the process. This may require them to be aggressive and manipulative, which is fine as long as they achieve their goal, which is make the sale at all costs. These are the people most responsible for creating the negative selling stigma that haunts customers, prospects and other salespeople alike.

Selling Style #2 (upper left)

THE FRIEND

The second selling style is the salesperson who goes into every interaction with ultimate goal of being seen as the customer's friend—even if it means losing the sale and leaving empty handed. The saddest thing about this selling style is they believe that not selling the customer is helping them, which of course, it isn't. These are the people most impacted by the negative selling stigma created by high-pressure salespeople because the last thing they want is for a prospect to think that's what *they* are. As a result, they function as "order takers" and are rarely proactive in any area except perhaps in "servicing" of accounts. They'll pass on the sale if it means they leave feeling good about themselves.

Selling Style #3 (lower left)

THE PRETENDER

This is the saddest selling style of all, because they have no objective other than being paid. They are simply *pretending* to be salespeople. The paycheck is all that matters—for as long as they can get it. Once you catch on that they are serving no one's interest other than their own, they're let go—only to land in another sales job for another unsuspecting employer. They bring NO redeeming value to anyone. The presence of Pretenders on your team is the ultimate lose/lose.

Selling Style #4 (upper right)

THE ADVISOR

Finally, we come to the ultimate of all selling styles: the person who goes into every interaction with the attitude that both parties must walk out winners for them to have done their job properly. Win/win is the only acceptable option. They ask great questions, determine needs, and once they have, they'll advise the customer to buy—which might require them to be assertive, but never aggressive. They believe that if the product/service being offered improves the customer's condition, they *go for no.* To take it a step further, when a true need has been established, they consider not selling the customer to be a *disservice.* As such, the trusted advisor model of selling is what all salespeople should strive to emulate.

Understanding these five selling styles and identifying which apply to the people on your team, is perhaps the single most important thing a leader can do to impact long-term sales.

The Five Failure Levels:

In our book, we share what we call, "The Five Failure Levels."

Level #1

The Ability to Fail

Everyone on planet earth has the ability to fail. It's where we all start! What keeps most people at level-one status is their intense desire to avoid any form of failure at all costs. As a result, 80% of all people never move past this basic level.

Level #2

The Willingness to Fail

Level-two people develop the willingness to fail, which means they come to accept failure as a natural by-product of the process of seeking success. Fewer than 20 percent of all people make it to Level #2 for any sustained period of time.

Level #3

The Wantingness to Fail

The biggest mental leap for most people is getting to a place where they stop tolerating NO as a necessary evil that must be dealt with in order to succeed, and they actually *want* to hear NO more often—where they develop the desire to increase the amount of failure they experience with the inner faith that personal and financial growth will follow. Fewer than 5 percent of all people ever get to level three.

Level #4

Failing Bigger and Faster

"Relax, I'm just practicing my bouncing back skills."

The people who ascend to level four are those who have come to the conclusion that if failing is good, then failing faster is better.

And not just failing faster—if one is going to increase their failure rate, they should do it going after big goals that are worthy of the effort.

Level #5

Failing Exponentially

This final level is a function of leadership through multiplication of effort. After all, if hearing NO more often can increase individual success, then getting everyone to fail more will lead to group (or team) success.

In part, doing this challenge will force you to move through each of these levels and when you do a challenge with as a team or as a leader, you can reach level five.

Conducting the Challenge

The 21 Day Go for No! Challenge contains a total of 7 steps.

The first 6 steps are for "pre-planning," with a final step to be completed once your challenge is over. In addition, be sure to check out the FAQs. (Have more questions? Join our Go for No! Community on Facebook or if you are a member of the course, ask us there.)

STEP ONE:

Decide How You Will Track Your NOs.

W. Clement Stone was the founder and president of Combined Insurance Company of America, and one of the greatest businessmen and philanthropists of the 20th century. Stone had an interesting and effective technique for helping new salespeople get over their fear of rejection. When training them, he would have them put 20 beans in one of their pockets. Then, to keep them from getting discouraged, he would tell them:

> *"When you get a NO from a prospect, move a bean from one pocket to the other. I promise that before all 20 beans have been moved, you'll get a sale."*

And he was usually right!

Stone understood that the quantity of calls was the key to success. It was also a great way to track their NOs and see how they led to yeses!

For the challenge to work, tracking and counting NOs is obviously critical.

- You need to know how many NOs you're hearing to know how many you collected during the challenge.
- Counting becomes the reminder to challenge yourself to collect more NOs.

It doesn't matter what you use to count and record your NOs. It only matters that you have some form of mechanism in place to track them.

If you are working at a desk and you have access to your daily tracking sheet in this workbook, great. Otherwise, track your NOs throughout the day and record them in this workbook later.

You can use hash marks on a piece of paper, a handheld counter, the notepad on your phone, or a pocketful of beans. Just make sure that you're counting the number of NOs you obtain during the day and that you're recording that number.

STEP TWO:

Set a NO-Goal™

Since you are probably used to setting traditional "yes" goals, this is not much different. The only difference is, instead of coming up with a goal for how many yeses you'll get, you are coming up with a goal for how many NOs you want to get.

A good place to start is to ask:

How many NOs are you getting on a regular basis now?

You could set a number based on what you already know about your business, or reverse engineer it. For example, if you wanted to get three yeses and you know you typically need to talk to 20 people to get those 3—you could set a no goal of 20. Or better yet, 30 so that you are striving to go beyond reaching your standard yes goal.

There are a few other considerations when it comes to setting a no-goal for the 21 Day period:

- You can set a no-goal for the entire 21 Day Challenge and then break it into 3 chunks, so you have a no-goal for each of the 3 weeks. For example, decide on a no-goal of 30 and then divide it by three so your goal is 10 NOs each week.
- You could use the ramp up method. For example, if your no-goal is 50 for the period, you could start with 10 for the first week and 20 for the next two weeks.
- Finally, you could hold off on setting a no-goal for the first week. Start counting your NOs for a week one to establish a baseline. Then based on what you were able to do, set a no-goal for weeks two and three.

Once you establish your no-goal, break it down by day. We have seen too many people set a no-goal and spend the last two days of the challenge racing to reach it. That is not the idea. You want to spread your activity over the 21 days and do something virtually every day.

As you can see, the no-goal process is flexible. We will not set one for you. And we do not recommend setting an arbitrary number like 100 – unless that is possible to achieve. If the no-goal is way out of reach, you will get discouraged and quit.

Once you have a number to shoot for, you are done. Just like going on a diet and exercise plan to lose weight, it is good to know the number you're shooting for. Once you do that, you quickly move on to focus on the behaviors necessary to achieve success, in this case, collecting NOs.

That brings us to the next step.

STEP THREE:

Get Prepared and Organized

Well before you start a challenge, you want to make sure you are fully prepared to start "going for no" on Day One. Sometimes people read *Go for No!* and they are so excited, they start a challenge immediately without any planning. We love the enthusiasm but getting yourself mentally prepared and physically organized will go a long way in your successful completion.

Mental Prep

The first aspect to this step is getting mentally prepared. Sometimes when people start a challenge, they get nervous at the last minute about being fully ready. While we do want you to get mentally prepared to begin, this does not mean more *training*. Whatever lack of skill or knowledge you feel you might lack, set that aside. Most people far underestimate what they are capable of because they let their limitations define what's possible. No one is perfect so instead of waiting until you are, get out there and see what you can do. Ignore the temptation to change your start date or worse, go back into "training mode."

Review your calendar and decide on the 21-day period for your challenge. Start whatever day of the week you want and pretty much any time. But, consider potential interruptions. Try not to involve too much else in your life during that time. Obviously, major holidays like Thanksgiving (in the US) through Christmas is a less than ideal time for a challenge. Stay focused and engaged. It is a short time frame but can create massive results in the long run.

The rest of the mental preparation comes from working through this guide, reading the FAQs and moving to the next aspect of this step which is to get physically organized.

Organization

Make sure you have all the components you need to execute your challenge. For example, you might need to:

- Update your CRM (if you use one) and/or get your contacts and spreadsheets in order.
- Make sure you have the files, messages/email templates, videos, links, demos and websites you could need and that they are working and easy to access.
- Ensure your phone, internet, website, etc. are working with no issues.
- Clean your desk and/or work area.
- If you are visiting prospects, clean your car, have all your clothes cleaned and ready.

See where we are going with this?

We don't want anything interfering or slowing you down during your challenge. There are enough interruptions and things that happen to knock people out of momentum so control what you can control.

Being organized feels good too. Whatever set up you need to feel ready and in control of your environment, knock that out before your start date.

It's amazing how much this physical preparation will do for your mindset and attitude. Once you've set your start and end date and you've gotten organized, you are ready!

STEP FOUR:
Create Dedicated Time to Go for No!

In order to ensure you hit your NO-Goal, you're going to need to spend more time *going for no*. But time is a limited and tightly controlled commodity. If we were asking you to spend money, you could dip into your bank account and pull out as much as you needed. But there is no such time account, is there?

Over the years, people have told us the biggest problem was not having blocked out specific times to go for no during the challenge. Of course, they *had* the time to go for no—they simply didn't make it their most important priority.

To increase the amount of time you spend going for no, you will need to determine what you're going to *stop doing* to free up the time. To start with, we suggest *batching* everything you do. That means for each project or task you have, batch those tasks into chunks so that you create more time to go for no. For example, we used to send our prospects physical packages by mail. Sometimes we'd run to the post office in the morning, and then have to run over again in the afternoon. Eventually we got smart and made it a rule to only go at the end of each afternoon. Simple time savings like this add up!

Also, put your Go for No! time on your calendar just like you would for any project, task or appointment. Don't let "running out of time" be your excuse for not hitting your NO-Goal. Schedule it—then stick to the schedule!

Finally, some tasks might just have to be put off entirely until AFTER the challenge is over. Getting your teeth cleaned is important, but they're not going to fall out of your head if you push it back a week or two. Need a new suit or dress? It can wait. And that movie you've been dying to see, don't worry—it will still be out three weeks from now. If not, you can catch it on Netflix (and for less money) a few months down the road.

Committing to making the time to go for no is fundamental to the success of your business and achieving your goals, so don't let the time get away from you. When the challenge is over, you can finish all the tasks you set aside. For right now, focus on the challenge!

STEP FIVE:
Start!

Yes, it seems rather obvious to include this as a step, but it is included because it is the most difficult. Psychologist Dr. David Viscott once said, *"If you can get up the courage to begin, you have the courage to succeed."*

Now you need the courage to begin. Normally the pressure and stress you place on yourself is to get a yes. In this case you should have zero pressure for any of that. The only pressure, if you want to call it that, is to try to hit the NO-Goal you've set.

It's critical that you celebrate your wins throughout the challenge period—in this case, we're talking about celebrating the NOs you collect. We hope you get plenty of yeses, of course, but you're probably doing an alright job of celebrating the yeses. But to keep yourself on an even keel, you need to be celebrating sales and prospecting activity *regardless of the outcome*. That means celebrating the sales you didn't make, too. And especially to celebrate when you hit your daily and/or weekly NO-Goal.

Celebrating your NOs not only reduces the highs and lows of the "emotional rollercoaster", it also starts the process of reprogramming the way you think when you experience rejection.

STEP SIX:

Get a NO-Buddy™

Technically, this step is optional, but important enough to include.

If you think it would aid you during your challenge, consider finding a NO-Buddy. This is someone to be accountable to during the challenge, who you can share your NO-goal, and report to at the end of each day or week. Just a quick text or call is enough of the accountability you need.

Your NO-Buddy can be anyone, but ideally this person would also be doing a challenge so you both have an equal interest in each other's success. Obviously, if there's someone on your team or in your office, they're the perfect candidate. That said, you don't need to be in the same business or industry – each of you out getting your NOs is enough!

If you thrive when partnering with others, this might be the difference between finishing and giving up. Finally, don't forget that you can always come into the private Facebook group that's part of our online course and find a NO-Buddy there. At a minimum, post your daily results for everyone to see and encourage you during your challenge.

STEP SEVEN:
Persist & Finish!

If starting was the most difficult, finishing is clearly the second hardest step in the challenge. But if you finish then you are in an elite group of people. So, finish. Or, as the disembodied voice whispered to Keven Costner in the movie *Field of Dreams*:

"Go the distance."

Business philosopher Jim Rohn said, *"The ultimate reason for setting goals is to entice you to become the person it takes to achieve them."*

During this challenge, any one day could feel like the perfect opportunity to throw in the towel. Like someone eating a cupcake in the middle of a weight loss challenge, you would never want them to quit the entire thing. Don't let the excuse of *"Well, I didn't go for no today so, I'm not going to finish the challenge,"* stall your progress. Just because you skip a day doesn't mean all the effort up until that moment has been wasted. Whatever happens… *keep going.*

Persist.

Finish the challenge!

FAQs

Here are some Frequently Asked Questions that can help you conduct a successful challenge:

Q: What Counts as a NO?

A: We realize that getting a hold of people is really challenging and people often want to make the getting of NOs easier. However…

- A voice mail message that you leave is NOT a no.
- A text or email that is not returned is NOT a no.
- "Let me think about it" is NOT a no.

We understand it's frustrating to be unable to "count" something as a no when often it may be. So, our rule for this is: in order to count something as a no without actually getting it verbally or through some other communication (text, email, etc.) you have to be sure that the person understands the offer they are saying no to and you need to have made an attempt a reasonable number of times.

Calling someone and leaving a message to set up a meeting is not a no. Even if they don't call you back. To decide something is a no in the first or second contact is not smart or practical. Our position is to make sure you have contacted someone multiple times before finally calling it a no. Granted, in 21 days you may find that it is harder to get a no because you have a shorter time frame to cultivate some connections and prospects in your pipeline today. No need to get frustrated by that, everything you do in this challenge, every contact, every connection, every person you speak with is all planting seeds for the future.

However tempting, don't count something as a no that really is not just to inflate your numbers. There may be a day where you had a lot of activity, but you still did not get any NOs. That should not discourage you, it's part of the process. You may find that you need to adjust your no goal so that you aren't always unable to reach it due to how long it takes you to get decisions from your prospects. And that is okay!

Q: How do I increase my NOs for the challenge?

Great question! And it is at the heart of what this challenge is all about. We encourage you to write down all the ways you can increase the NOs in your particular business. Examples to get you thinking:

- Prospecting for new customers.
- Following up with people in your existing pipeline. This should include people who said no in the past.
- Expanding the sale with new and existing customers. What are the new products, upgrades, or improvements they should know about?
- Add-ons to a sale of additional products and services. When we were in the retail industry, we called this selling Up, Down, Across and Sideways.
- Contacting happy clients for referrals.

Be creative. It's up to you to figure out all your Go for No! Moments and then execute on all those opportunities.

Q: How do I avoid coming across pushy during the challenge?

A key concept of going for no is, no doesn't mean never, no means not yet. Are we suggesting you turn into a pushy aggressive sales type badgering people over and over? Of course not. A no is always a perfectly acceptable answer. So, if you are looking for tricks or aggressive manipulation to force people who don't want or need what you have, we think you'll agree we never suggest that. The answer to not being pushy is, don't be pushy. That said, you can ask specific, thoughtful questions that could help people see things a different way. Perhaps someone who thinks they don't need your product or service simply does not understand it. And that leads us to the next question…

Q: Should I be trying to turn a NO into a YES?

Turning a no into a yes is a skill which absolutely can be done. Whether you want to try depends what kind of a no you are talking about and the circumstances of the interaction. Occasionally people will give you the reason behind the no. In other words, they will share their objection with you. But most often you'll have no idea. If you have the opportunity and you want to probe further, do it. In the simplest way, ask why they said no.

Whether there is a timing issue, a misunderstanding about the price or a product feature, or the person is happy with another provider – all give you an opportunity to keep the conversation going, even if it's next week or next month. Remember what your intention is (the intention is coming from a sell is to serve standpoint.) Be curious and gather information, never by being pushy. Everything you can learn will help you with the current prospect and for others in the future.

Finally, if the reason they said no is something completely out of your control and it's a no that could never be a yes, that's good too. A good no is always better than a bad yes. Plus, it's much better to get a no rather than have a bunch of false opportunities clogging up your pipeline.

Q: Should I tell people they can give me a NO?

It's one thing to have a Go for No! mindset but asking for a no might seem like sabotage. As you probably have experienced, people typically shy away from telling salespeople, no. If you find that someone is not getting back to you and they are avoiding you like the plague, asking for a no might be the way to finally get an answer.

You can let someone know that no is a perfectly acceptable answer and it's cool; if it's a no, it's no big deal. You are busy and you don't want to waste their time or your own. The irony is, when you become comfortable with doing this, it tends to attract people far more than you realize. Sometimes just removing all pressure will be the thing that gets people curious and more interested to hear you out. So, don't be afraid of making no an option for people to take. Your lack of fear of being rejected is one of the absolute best ways you can demonstrate confidence in yourself and in what you have to offer. Just because someone says no today doesn't mean you can't pursue that NO later.

Q: What if I get nothing but NOs during this challenge?

Obviously, the point of the challenge is through the gathering of NOs, the yeses will emerge. But if indeed you are getting nothing but NO, you must analyze your strategy. Step back and ask, where am I going wrong? How is my approach? How is my presentation? And most key: are you talking to qualified prospects? If not, it likely could be part of the issue. Or, maybe you are getting a lot of people to say yes to an initial meeting but have a hard time when it comes time to close the deal, getting NOs at the end of the process.

The good news is, when you start increasing your numbers, you start getting great data! You can't effectively analyze where your opportunity to improve is, if you don't have enough information to rely on. So, make small changes. Mix up your approach. See what happens. Still nothing but NOs? Change something else. Try. Test. Experiment. It's one of the great ways that you make going for no work for you.

But remember this too, like any MLB hitter, sometimes you just get into a slump. Don't panic. If you've analyzed where you need to improve and you're making those changes, just keep getting to the plate and swinging!

Q: What if I still have a fear of rejection?

Most people will have initial discomfort and fear. Some may have a great deal of it. If your current state is to fear a 'NO' the answer is not to wait it out. The fear will be there, challenge or not. And the fear won't necessarily go away, at least not immediately.

Your fear is not bad or good, it just is. Your brain thinks it's helping to protect you. It thinks you need this type of fear to survive. Start challenging your brain a little.

Ask yourself: What am I really afraid of?

If it's that you are afraid of hearing NO, which maybe up until his point you were, you are now going for no, so that fear is irrelevant. Thank your brain for trying to help you out and then take action. When you start, be excited about the possibilities and leave the fear of NO behind. That's what you are trying to achieve right?

Q: How can I maintain a positive mindset when getting a lot of NOs?

Past programming might make you feel like all the NOs should be depressing. We see it as a ton of great activity and something to celebrate. Remember, the celebrate part in section on starting?

But of course, you always want to be putting good stuff into your mind. Listen to your favorite speakers and experts and read good books. We listen to stuff all the time. Some of our favorites are Tom Bilyeu, Lewis Howes, Rachel and Dave Hollis, Marisa Peer, and Trevor Moawad, to name just a few. We also have a page in Amazon with all of our go-to recommendations at https://www.amazon.com/shop/goforno.

And of course, when it comes to Go for No, we highly suggest you get into our course and get engaged into our private Facebook group. It's a great place to share what's going on with you and get support during a challenge! You've heard of motivation? We do *NOtivation.*

Q: What if I am self-conscious about selling to someone who is higher in "status" or more successful than I am?

First, remember that no matter who you are and what you do, you are selling to humans. You might be a high school dropout selling supplies to a successful physician, but they are still human. No one is perfect and everyone suffers from the same issues as everyone else. You are worthwhile. End of story. That said, your job is to sell the value of the product, service, or idea – not the "value" of you. That means you can't look for validation of who you are as a person inside a sale. It's easy to fall into the trap of transferring your perceived personal status onto what it is you are selling and feel you can't measure up. So, if a homeless person discovered a Picasso in the trash, could they not sell it to a millionaire?

But what if you ARE the product? An actor, consultant or a personal chef all sell themselves and their skills. It's a fair concern. And if you are selling services like those, you do need to work on improving your skills so that you can increase your value to the marketplace to justify having successful ("high status") clients as well as higher fees. If you have a "growth mindset" you believe that you can always keep getting better, grow your value for your clients, and that you are not stuck. You can become among the best there is in your profession.

■

We are biologically wired to avoid being rejected. But we are also wired for persistence, perseverance and overcoming adversity.

Both are in our DNA. We get to choose which to act on. Rejection can break you down for good or it can mold you into something stronger.

■

Tour of the Daily Tracking Sheet

Here are the 10 elements of the 21 Day Go for No! Challenge Daily Tracking Sheet:

1) Day of the week and date (self-explanatory).
2) Previous NOs collected (starts with "zero" on Day 1) and accumulates each day going forward.
3) Today's NO-Goals:
    a. One for "business/work" NOs (sales calls, recruiting attempts, etc.)
    b. And a second goal for number of "personal" NOs you want to collect for the new day (example: requesting a free upgrade at a hotel, a better table in a restaurant, asking your kids to clean up their room.)
4) Tally your NOs in each of the above categories, via hashmarks as you go, or entered at the end of each day.
5) The total of all NOs to date, adding lines 2 (previous NOs) and line 4 (collected that day) together, done for both your Business and Personal NOs.
6) Identify at least one "Big Fish" you intend to prospect/attempt to approach with your offer. This might be a "High Value" prospect that represents an above average dollar/unit sale opportunity or a person with a higher title/position than you usually call on.
7) Identify a client or prospect you most need to "follow up" with, perhaps someone you've been putting off for a while.
8) Another great way to increase your NOs is to use the "One More Call" approach by adopting the habit (at the normal end of your day, when you're ready to go home) to dial the phone one more time or to knock on one more door—even if it's a prospect you believe is going to say NO to you. Making "one more call" every day, 5 days a week, means 200+ extra calls per year!
9) Rate yourself on your Go for No! effort for the day, from "poor" to "excellent."
10) Finally, make notes about your day and any observations about how going for no is affecting your attitude about failure and rejection, and the results you're experiencing by intentionally increasing and tracking your NOs.

As you see, the magic of this challenge is in its simplicity, not its complexity.

21 Day Go for No!® Challenge: DAY

1	Day of Week:		Date:	
2	Previous Business NOs Collected:		Previous Personal NOs Collected:	
3	Today's Business NO-Goal™:		Today's Personal NO-Goal™:	
4	<u>Business</u> NOs Collected Today:		<u>Personal</u> NOs Collected Today:	
5	TOTAL <u>Business</u> NOs To Date:		TOTAL <u>Personal</u> NOs To Date:	

6	Today's "BIG FISH":	7	Today's Critical FOLLOW UP:
8	Today's "ONE MORE CALL":	9	Today's GFN Effort Rating: <<<< Poor OK Excellent >>>> 1 2 3 4 5 6 7 8 9 10

10	Misc. Notes & Observations:

■

In a Go for No Moment you have 2 choices:

1) Don't ask, they'll just say no.

2) Have to ask to get either a yes or no.

Which one will lead to more yeses?

■

The 21 Day
Go for No!®
Challenge

Starts Here →

Daily NOtivation™

Everyone loves the sound of the word, YES! It's so positive, so empowering. And then there's NO. For most people, NO is just the opposite—negative, draining, the antithesis of YES. But what if everyone's wrong? What if NO could actually be the most empowering word in the world? What if you could achieve every quota, reach every income goal, an achieve every dream by simply learning to hear NO more often?

Well, you can.

21 Day Go for No!® Challenge: DAY 1

1	Day of Week:	Date:
2	Previous Business NOs Collected: 0	Previous Personal NOs Collected: 0
3	Today's Business NO-Goal™:	Today's Personal NO-Goal™:
4	Business NOs Collected Today:	Personal NOs Collected Today:
5	TOTAL Business NOs To Date:	TOTAL Personal NOs To Date:

6 Today's "BIG FISH":

7 Today's Critical FOLLOW UP:

8 Today's "ONE MORE CALL":

9 Today's GFN Effort Rating:

<<<< Poor OK Excellent >>>>

1 2 3 4 5 6 7 8 9 10

10 Misc. Notes & Observations:

Daily NOtivation™

You must get beyond the "willingness" to tolerate 'NO' and learn to embrace it!

■

You can achieve virtually anything you want if you're just willing to hear 'NO' often enough.

■

The reason someone says 'YES' or 'NO' to your offer rarely has anything to do with *you* as a person. Never take 'NO' personally. 'NO' isn't personal.

21 Day Go for No!® Challenge: DAY 2

1	Day of Week:	Date:	
2	Previous Business NOs Collected:	Previous Personal NOs Collected:	
3	Today's Business NO-Goal™:	Today's Personal NO-Goal™:	
4	Business NOs Collected Today:	Personal NOs Collected Today:	
5	TOTAL Business NOs To Date:	TOTAL Personal NOs To Date:	
6	Today's "BIG FISH":	7	Today's Critical FOLLOW UP:
8	Today's "ONE MORE CALL":	9	Today's GFN Effort Rating: <<<< Poor OK Excellent >>>> 1 2 3 4 5 6 7 8 9 10
10	Misc. Notes & Observations:		

Daily NOtivation™

To achieve meaningful success—to be considered successful by virtually any standard—you must be willing to fail. There are NO exceptions to this rule.

■

No matter what you're selling—regardless of how poorly or how well you presented the offer—some people are going to say NO to you. *So what?*

■

Remember: It takes no more energy to get a BIG NO than to get a small one. After all, NO is a NO is a NO—NO matter who it's coming from.

21 Day Go for No!® Challenge: DAY 3

1	Day of Week:	Date:
2	Previous Business NOs Collected:	Previous Personal NOs Collected:
3	Today's Business NO-Goal™:	Today's Personal NO-Goal™:
4	Business NOs Collected Today:	Personal NOs Collected Today:
5	TOTAL Business NOs To Date:	TOTAL Personal NOs To Date:
6	Today's "BIG FISH":	
7	Today's Critical FOLLOW UP:	
8	Today's "ONE MORE CALL":	
9	Today's GFN Effort Rating: <<<< Poor OK Excellent >>>> 1 2 3 4 5 6 7 8 9 10	
10	Misc. Notes & Observations:	

Daily NOtivation™

Having YES-Goals is important but having NO-Goals™ is critical.

■

Don't prejudge anyone, ever. Give everyone the opportunity to say 'NO' to you because if you don't, you're simply saying NO to yourself. If someone else rejects you, okay, but to reject yourself?

■

93% of successful people say they learned more from their failures than from their successes. What do they know that you don't?

21 Day Go for No!® Challenge: DAY 4

1	Day of Week:		Date:	
2	Previous Business NOs Collected:		Previous Personal NOs Collected:	
3	Today's Business NO-Goal™:		Today's Personal NO-Goal™:	
4	Business NOs Collected Today:		Personal NOs Collected Today:	
5	TOTAL Business NOs To Date:		TOTAL Personal NOs To Date:	
6	Today's "BIG FISH":	7	Today's Critical FOLLOW UP:	
8	Today's "ONE MORE CALL":	9	Today's GFN Effort Rating: <<<< Poor OK Excellent >>>> 1 2 3 4 5 6 7 8 9 10	
10	Misc. Notes & Observations:			

Daily NOtivation™

Go for No!* is a process—a *tool*—that can be used to club a prospect over the head when in the wrong hands, but also one that can be used to create a win-win sale when in the customer's best interest. To be clear: this is the ONLY way you should ever *go for no.

■

Don't take 'NO' personally. The reason why someone says NO to you today will be the exact reason someone else will say YES to you tomorrow. It's not about you, it's about them.

21 Day Go for No!® Challenge: DAY 5

1	Day of Week:	Date:
2	Previous Business NOs Collected:	Previous Personal NOs Collected:
3	Today's Business NO-Goal™:	Today's Personal NO-Goal™:
4	Business NOs Collected Today:	Personal NOs Collected Today:
5	TOTAL Business NOs To Date:	TOTAL Personal NOs To Date:

6	Today's "BIG FISH":	7	Today's Critical FOLLOW UP:
8	Today's "ONE MORE CALL":	9	Today's GFN Effort Rating: <<<< Poor OK Excellent >>>> 1 2 3 4 5 6 7 8 9 10

10	Misc. Notes & Observations:

Daily NOtivation™

Going for 'NO' requires you to surrender your old belief that if you fail, that *you* are failure. Failure is an *event*, not a person.

■

You must abandon the notion that the best way to increase your success is to decrease your failure. The best way to increase your success is increase your FAILURE.

■

If failure is a vehicle that can take you to success, then courage is the fuel.

21 Day Go for No!® Challenge: DAY 6

1	Day of Week:	Date:
2	Previous Business NOs Collected:	Previous Personal NOs Collected:
3	Today's Business NO-Goal™:	Today's Personal NO-Goal™:
4	<u>Business</u> NOs Collected Today:	<u>Personal</u> NOs Collected Today:
5	TOTAL <u>Business</u> NOs To Date:	TOTAL <u>Personal</u> NOs To Date:

6	Today's "BIG FISH":	7	Today's Critical FOLLOW UP:
8	Today's "ONE MORE CALL":	9	Today's GFN Effort Rating: <<<< Poor OK Excellent >>>> 1 2 3 4 5 6 7 8 9 10

10	Misc. Notes & Observations:

Daily NOtivation™

The choice is never between success or failure. It's always success and failure.

■

If you're not achieving the level of success you want, you're probably not failing enough.

■

Failure and rejection don't have to be debilitating. By reprogramming yourself to think differently, failure and rejection can become powerful positives in your life.

21 Day Go for No!® Challenge: DAY 7

1	Day of Week:		Date:	
2	Previous Business NOs Collected:		Previous Personal NOs Collected:	
3	Today's Business NO-Goal™:		Today's Personal NO-Goal™:	
4	<u>Business</u> NOs Collected Today:		<u>Personal</u> NOs Collected Today:	
5	TOTAL <u>Business</u> NOs To Date:		TOTAL <u>Personal</u> NOs To Date:	

6	Today's "BIG FISH":	7	Today's Critical FOLLOW UP:
8	Today's "ONE MORE CALL":	9	Today's GFN Effort Rating: <<<< Poor OK Excellent >>>> 1 2 3 4 5 6 7 8 9 10
10	Misc. Notes & Observations:		

Daily NOtivation™

The fear of the word 'NO' is the only thing standing between most people and greatness.

■

What would happen if you decided to make each 'NO' you encountered was something that empowered you and made you stronger?

■

Don't forget to ask for referrals. It's another important way to increase the quantity of NOs you're getting.

21 Day Go for No!® Challenge: DAY 8

1	Day of Week:	Date:	
2	Previous Business NOs Collected:		Previous Personal NOs Collected:	
3	Today's Business NO-Goal™:		Today's Personal NO-Goal™:	
4	Business NOs Collected Today:		Personal NOs Collected Today:	
5	TOTAL Business NOs To Date:		TOTAL Personal NOs To Date:	

6	Today's "BIG FISH":	7	Today's Critical FOLLOW UP:
8	Today's "ONE MORE CALL":	9	Today's GFN Effort Rating: <<<< Poor OK Excellent >>>> 1 2 3 4 5 6 7 8 9 10
10	Misc. Notes & Observations:		

Daily NOtivation™

Remember the SW/SW/SW/SW principle: *Some will. Some won't. So what? Someone's waiting!*

■

Going for 'NO' is not "negative thinking." It's learning to take something most people perceive as negative and turning it into a powerful positive.

■

When you hit a streak of yeses, the worst thing you can do is to slack off and stop selling. After all, when you're hot, you're hot—so keep going for 'NO.'

21 Day Go for No!® Challenge: DAY 9

1	Day of Week:		Date:	
2	Previous Business NOs Collected:		Previous Personal NOs Collected:	
3	Today's Business NO-Goal™:		Today's Personal NO-Goal™:	
4	Business NOs Collected Today:		Personal NOs Collected Today:	
5	TOTAL Business NOs To Date:		TOTAL Personal NOs To Date:	

6	Today's "BIG FISH":	7	Today's Critical FOLLOW UP:
8	Today's "ONE MORE CALL":	9	Today's GFN Effort Rating: <<<< Poor OK Excellent >>>> 1 2 3 4 5 6 7 8 9 10
10	Misc. Notes & Observations:		

Daily NOtivation™

Never make assumptions about what someone will decide, do, or spend. Your next call, meeting, or appointment might be a 'NO', but it might also be a YES that could change your life.

Never prejudge anyone. Ever.

■

When you see the sign marked "failure," *don't stop*—success is usually straight ahead.

■

The salesperson never decides when the sale is over, only the customer.

21 Day Go for No!® Challenge: DAY 10

1	Day of Week:		Date:
2	Previous Business NOs Collected:		Previous Personal NOs Collected:
3	Today's Business NO-Goal™:		Today's Personal NO-Goal™:
4	Business NOs Collected Today:		Personal NOs Collected Today:
5	TOTAL Business NOs To Date:		TOTAL Personal NOs To Date:
6	Today's "BIG FISH":	7	Today's Critical FOLLOW UP:
8	Today's "ONE MORE CALL":	9	Today's GFN Effort Rating: <<<< Poor OK Excellent >>>> 1 2 3 4 5 6 7 8 9 10
10	Misc. Notes & Observations:		

Daily NOtivation™

Hearing yes is the easy part of the job and teaches you virtually nothing. Learning to hear 'NO' over and over again and to never quit is what builds character and self-esteem.

■

Failing and *being a failure* are two very different things. Successful people fail eagerly and often, while failures avoid failing.

■

If no one has said 'NO' to you today you're playing things way too safe.

21 Day Go for No!® Challenge: DAY 11

1	Day of Week:	Date:
2	Previous Business NOs Collected:	Previous Personal NOs Collected:
3	Today's Business NO-Goal™:	Today's Personal NO-Goal™:
4	Business NOs Collected Today:	Personal NOs Collected Today:
5	TOTAL Business NOs To Date:	TOTAL Personal NOs To Date:
6	Today's "BIG FISH":	7 Today's Critical FOLLOW UP:
8	Today's "ONE MORE CALL":	9 Today's GFN Effort Rating: <<<< Poor OK Excellent >>>> 1 2 3 4 5 6 7 8 9 10
10	Misc. Notes & Observations:	

Daily <u>NO</u>tivation™

Remember: NO doesn't mean never.

NO means not yet.

■

If you truly want to accelerate your performance, you need to start failing more, and failing faster!

■

There is a big difference between failing and *being* a failure. The only way to <u>be</u> a failure is to quit.

21 Day Go for No!® Challenge: DAY 12

1	Day of Week:	Date:
2	Previous Business NOs Collected:	Previous Personal NOs Collected:
3	Today's Business NO-Goal™:	Today's Personal NO-Goal™:
4	Business NOs Collected Today:	Personal NOs Collected Today:
5	TOTAL Business NOs To Date:	TOTAL Personal NOs To Date:
6 / 7	Today's "BIG FISH":	Today's Critical FOLLOW UP:
8 / 9	Today's "ONE MORE CALL":	Today's GFN Effort Rating: <<<< Poor OK Excellent >>>> 1 2 3 4 5 6 7 8 9 10
10	Misc. Notes & Observations:	

Daily NOtivation™

The shortest distance between YOU and SUCCESS is on a straight line, never on an up and down, emotional roller coaster.

■

Make "going for no" a priority by scheduling time to do it. There is no such thing as trying to find time—make it!

■

Invite your fear to sit down and thank it for helping keep you safe from real danger. Remind it that asking for a sale isn't real danger, it's only *imagined* danger.

21 Day Go for No!® Challenge: DAY 13

1	Day of Week:		Date:	
2	Previous Business NOs Collected:		Previous Personal NOs Collected:	
3	Today's Business NO-Goal™:		Today's Personal NO-Goal™:	
4	<u>Business</u> NOs Collected Today:		<u>Personal</u> NOs Collected Today:	
5	TOTAL <u>Business</u> NOs To Date:		TOTAL <u>Personal</u> NOs To Date:	

6	Today's "BIG FISH":	7	Today's Critical FOLLOW UP:
8	Today's "ONE MORE CALL":	9	Today's GFN Effort Rating: <<<< Poor OK Excellent >>>> 1 2 3 4 5 6 7 8 9 10

10	Misc. Notes & Observations:

Daily NOtivation™

Numbing yourself to NO isn't about ignoring it—it's about experiencing it so often that it eventually loses its power over you.

■

When someone tells you 'NO,' the next thing you do is ask… *"Why?"*

■

Never let a 'NO' deject you. You could be just one 'NO' (and one YES) away from finding your next life changing yes.

21 Day Go for No!® Challenge: DAY 14

1	Day of Week:	Date:
2	Previous Business NOs Collected:	Previous Personal NOs Collected:
3	Today's Business NO-Goal™:	Today's Personal NO-Goal™:
4	Business NOs Collected Today:	Personal NOs Collected Today:
5	TOTAL Business NOs To Date:	TOTAL Personal NOs To Date:
6	Today's "BIG FISH":	7 Today's Critical FOLLOW UP:
8	Today's "ONE MORE CALL":	9 Today's GFN Effort Rating: <<<< Poor OK Excellent >>>> 1 2 3 4 5 6 7 8 9 10
10	Misc. Notes & Observations:	

Daily NOtivation™

When average people hear "NO" they think the process is over. When top performers hear "NO" they think things are just getting started.

■

Don't be afraid to go for a bigger "NO" than you think is possible. Stretch your thinking about the most ridiculous, you-will-almost-certainly-get-a-'NO' prospect you can imagine, and just go for it. Because, who knows?

21 Day Go for No!® Challenge: DAY 15

1	Day of Week:	Date:
2	Previous Business NOs Collected:	Previous Personal NOs Collected:
3	Today's Business NO-Goal™:	Today's Personal NO-Goal™:
4	Business NOs Collected Today:	Personal NOs Collected Today:
5	TOTAL Business NOs To Date:	TOTAL Personal NOs To Date:

6	Today's "BIG FISH":	7	Today's Critical FOLLOW UP:
8	Today's "ONE MORE CALL":	9	Today's GFN Effort Rating: <<<< Poor OK Excellent >>>> 1 2 3 4 5 6 7 8 9 10

10	Misc. Notes & Observations:

Daily NOtivation™

No one is born with the fear of rejection—rejection is learned. And anything learned can be unlearned.

■

The secret to sales success can be summed up in one word: *Ask.*

■

Accept the idea that 'NO' is a perfectly acceptable answer. It may not be the answer you want, but you must learn to be okay with it.

21 Day Go for No!® Challenge: DAY 16

1	Day of Week:	Date:
2	Previous Business NOs Collected:	Previous Personal NOs Collected:
3	Today's Business NO-Goal™:	Today's Personal NO-Goal™:
4	Business NOs Collected Today:	Personal NOs Collected Today:
5	TOTAL Business NOs To Date:	TOTAL Personal NOs To Date:

6	Today's "BIG FISH":	7	Today's Critical FOLLOW UP:
8	Today's "ONE MORE CALL":	9	Today's GFN Effort Rating: <<<< Poor OK Excellent >>>> 1 2 3 4 5 6 7 8 9 10

10	Misc. Notes & Observations:

Daily NOtivation™

A study of 1,126 inbound customer inquiries to a corporate call center showed that when salespeople failed to 'ask for the order' customers still bought 17% of the time! When salespeople *did* ask for the order, the closure rate DOUBLED to an impressive 41%.

But when salespeople asked the same customer TWICE for the sale, the closure rate skyrocketed to 81%!

Source: ***ContactPoint, St. Georges, Utah***

21 Day Go for No!® Challenge: DAY 17

1	Day of Week:	Date:
2	Previous Business NOs Collected:	Previous Personal NOs Collected:
3	Today's Business NO-Goal™:	Today's Personal NO-Goal™:
4	Business NOs Collected Today:	Personal NOs Collected Today:
5	TOTAL Business NOs To Date:	TOTAL Personal NOs To Date:

6 Today's "BIG FISH":

7 Today's Critical FOLLOW UP:

8 Today's "ONE MORE CALL":

9 Today's GFN Effort Rating:

<<<< Poor OK Excellent >>>>

1 2 3 4 5 6 7 8 9 10

10 Misc. Notes & Observations:

Daily NOtivation™

When you *go for no* you are not hoping wishing or praying for a NO. You are not sabotaging yourself or doing a poor job of selling or prospecting. You aren't hanging up on people who call you and are ready to place an order. That really would be sabotaging yourself, wouldn't it? Ultimately, the goal is to get a yes, and with enough NOs you will collect plenty of them.

■

Yes is the destination.
NO is how you get there.

21 Day Go for No!® Challenge: DAY 18

1	Day of Week:		Date:	
2	Previous Business NOs Collected:		Previous Personal NOs Collected:	
3	Today's Business NO-Goal™:		Today's Personal NO-Goal™:	
4	Business NOs Collected Today:		Personal NOs Collected Today:	
5	TOTAL Business NOs To Date:		TOTAL Personal NOs To Date:	
6	Today's "BIG FISH":	7	Today's Critical FOLLOW UP:	
8	Today's "ONE MORE CALL":	9	Today's GFN Effort Rating: <<<< Poor OK Excellent >>>> 1 2 3 4 5 6 7 8 9 10	
10	Misc. Notes & Observations:			

Daily NOtivation™

Contrary to what you've heard, opportunity doesn't knock—you knock, and opportunity answers. Unfortunately, when it does, it sometimes says, "NO!"

■

Never over-complicate a follow up call that you know you should have made long ago. Just tell the truth and say, *"I dropped the ball."*

Start there, then see where the conversation goes.

21 Day Go for No!® Challenge: DAY 19

1	Day of Week:		Date:	
2	Previous Business NOs Collected:		Previous Personal NOs Collected:	
3	Today's Business NO-Goal™:		Today's Personal NO-Goal™:	
4	Business NOs Collected Today:		Personal NOs Collected Today:	
5	TOTAL Business NOs To Date:		TOTAL Personal NOs To Date:	
6	Today's "BIG FISH":	7	Today's Critical FOLLOW UP:	
8	Today's "ONE MORE CALL":	9	Today's GFN Effort Rating: <<<< Poor OK Excellent >>>> 1 2 3 4 5 6 7 8 9 10	
10	Misc. Notes & Observations:			

Daily **NO**tivation™

Going for 'NO' is an opportunity to serve others with your product, service, or idea. As long as you understand that you never have to feel guilty about asking for the sale.

■

Never look at a 'NO' as being negative. Look at it as a gift that, if unwrapped and examined, contains the information you need to move forward.

■

***Remember:* When done right, to "sell" is to "serve."**

21 Day Go for No!® Challenge: DAY 20

1	Day of Week:		Date:	
2	Previous Business NOs Collected:		Previous Personal NOs Collected:	
3	Today's Business NO-Goal™:		Today's Personal NO-Goal™:	
4	Business NOs Collected Today:		Personal NOs Collected Today:	
5	TOTAL Business NOs To Date:		TOTAL Personal NOs To Date:	

6	Today's "BIG FISH":	7	Today's Critical FOLLOW UP:
8	Today's "ONE MORE CALL":	9	Today's GFN Effort Rating: <<<< Poor OK Excellent >>>> 1 2 3 4 5 6 7 8 9 10

10	Misc. Notes & Observations:

Daily NOtivation™

44% of all people give up after hearing "NO" one time...

22% more give up after the 2nd "NO"...

14% more give up after the 3rd "NO"...

12% more give up after the 4th "NO"...

Yet, 60% of all customers say "NO" four times before finally saying YES.

■

Remember, easy yeses produce little successes. Go for BIGGER NOs!

21 Day Go for No!® Challenge: DAY 21

1	Day of Week:	Date:
2	Previous Business NOs Collected:	Previous Personal NOs Collected:
3	Today's Business NO-Goal™:	Today's Personal NO-Goal™:
4	Business NOs Collected Today:	Personal NOs Collected Today:
5	TOTAL Business NOs To Date:	TOTAL Personal NOs To Date:

6	Today's "BIG FISH":	7	Today's Critical FOLLOW UP:
8	Today's "ONE MORE CALL":	9	Today's GFN Effort Rating: <<<< Poor OK Excellent >>>> 1 2 3 4 5 6 7 8 9 10

10	Misc. Notes & Observations:

Review Your Results

Congratulations on completing the challenge! Here are some questions to consider and a space to jot down some final notes regarding your observations and what you learned from the 21-day experience.

First, the BIG question: Did your performance improve as a result of *"going for no"* for 21 days?

YES / NO

Did you hit the NO-Goals you set for yourself? If not, why not?

____

____

____

Did you find the NO-Goals you set for yourself during the challenge were too difficult to hit? Or too easy? And why?

____

____

____

Did you include some personal NO-Goals along the way, things that were totally unrelated to selling or business? If so, what good things came from doing this?

____

____

____

Did you find yourself forgetting to go for no from time to time? If so, how can you become more NO-Goal focused in the future?

____

____

____

Do you feel you truly challenged yourself to step outside your comfort zone? If not, why?

____

____

____

What was your biggest take away that you learned during the challenge?

____

____

____

What are you most proud of yourself for achieving during the challenge?

____

____

____

Lastly, what if your results were not at the level you expected? Robert Louis Stevenson said, *"Don't judge each day by the harvest you reap but by the seeds that you plant."* For some of you, your results will trickle in over the weeks and months from this challenge. Think about the seeds *you* have planted in just 21 days by going for no.

Extra Daily Tracking Sheet "Master"

Here's an additional blank MASTER COPY of the Daily Tracking Sheet.

Feel free to make photocopies should you wish to conduct an additional *Go for No!® Challenge.*

21 Day Go for No!® Challenge: DAY

1	Day of Week:	Date:
2	Previous Business NOs Collected:	Previous Personal NOs Collected:
3	Today's Business NO-Goal™:	Today's Personal NO-Goal™:
4	Business NOs Collected Today:	Personal NOs Collected Today:
5	TOTAL Business NOs To Date:	TOTAL Personal NOs To Date:

6	Today's "BIG FISH":	7	Today's Critical FOLLOW UP:
8	Today's "ONE MORE CALL":	9	Today's GFN Effort Rating: <<<< Poor OK Excellent >>>> 1 2 3 4 5 6 7 8 9 10

10	Misc. Notes & Observations:

Bonus Inspiration from

The Go for No!® Movie

For more information on *The Go for No! Movie* and to watch the trailer, visit https://goforno.cinevee.com/

If I can deal with 7 to 10 NOs, I'm going to make $500. So, I divided the $500 by 10, to receive 10 NOs, did you hear my language? To *receive* 10 NOs. Like, what a pleasure to get a "NO!" Because I just made $50. So, I taped the $50 bill to my phone and every time I picked it up, and made a cold call, or any kind of prospecting call and received a "No," as soon as I hung it up, it was, "Thanks for the 50 bucks!" That really transformed my mindset about the word "NO."

-Lisa Jimenez

If someone hears the word "NO" and they retreat, it probably wasn't that important to them. If they hear the word "NO" and they treat it as "not yet, then the question becomes, *"What are you willing to do?"* You have to accept the fact that the word "NO" is part of life. I often tell people that there are no boundaries, no parameters. There are no rules or regulations unless you choose to place them there. The good news is that when you bust through your own mental boundaries, it's not called trespassing.

-Jeff Blackman

I think the best way to deal with failure is not to give up. It's OK to have a little pity party, it's OK to get in the corner and cry for half an hour, but sooner or later you must rise and you must say, "I will do this again. I will not let this be the end of it all. There is a rainbow at the end of all of this, and I may have to listen to one, two, three, four or five NOs before I get to the 'maybe' and I get to the yes." Had I really given up, had I believed that "NO" meant the end of the world, I think I would have taken a completely different course in life. And that may not have been as good as the one that I've been blessed with.

-Nido Qubein

The word, NO, I call it feedback. Now, you know one more way that doesn't work, one more way that doesn't work. You've got feedback, and you might try a lot of them, but the only way that you can really fail is if you give in to that. It's that idea of picking yourself up and dusting yourself off, of completing the race. There is no failure unless you allow it to be that for you by quitting.

-Margie Aliprandi

Failure is learning—you learn from failure. Failure is a tool. I didn't learn from winning. I learned from failure. How are you going to learn if you don't fail?

-Rudy Ruettiger

The prize in direct proportion to the price - what comes easy is worth very little, what comes hard is worth so much. So, the NOs are so wonderful because they're making you so much better. I always taught that selling is really a law of averages, that there's a certain number of NOs that you need to get to yeses. If I had to summarize all the sales companies I've worked with and had to pick a number, I would guess it would be one out of five, that in almost all selling situations it takes five people before you get a yes. That means 80 percent is saying, "NO," and 20 percent is saying "yes." If it's a high paying sales job, it usually has to be that way, because if everybody said, "yes," they wouldn't need to pay you very well. So, you really get paid for the NOs not the yeses.

-Joel Weldon

I think when people hear "No" it's sort of like the green light, yellow light, red light. When people hear "No," the majority of people they see the red light. Stop. Go no further. Failure. Rejection. That's where they end things when they hear the word "No." Me, the way I was brought up, I was brought up on the philosophy if you don't ask, you don't get. And if you don't get, ask again - maybe they misunderstood the question!

-Tony Alessandra

I basically grew up a salesperson, that's what I did my whole life. I sold telephone systems, and I sold speeches. That's why I was so successful in the speaking industry. Very early on, I asked everybody to buy. I mean *everybody* to buy. If they had any money, I was going to ask them if they wanted me to come and speak. It's the oldest sales cliché in the world, *"Every 'NO' gets you closer to a yes,"* but those clichés are clichés for a reason—they work some of the time, and that one does. So, I would just laugh and say, "OK, well," all the way to the next yes. That really was how I looked at it.

There are more bad salespeople selling bad products at a higher price than there are good salespeople selling good products at a reasonable price. The bad salespeople can make more money (which might make them good salespeople) simply because they ask more people. They just stay with it all of the time. They don't understand what rejection is. They look at rejection as a challenge.

-Larry Winget

I don't know if I've truly ever heard the word 'NO.' To be honest with you, I don't think it registers in my mind. I nagged my parents, nagged, persisted, to get a puppy. They said, 'No. Laura, no. You're not old enough. We can't do this. You're not going to take care of it.' 'But why not?' 'No, Laura.' Well guess what? I broke through. I got them to go look at the puppy. I got them to go look at it. They still said 'NO.' 'But you guys I want a puppy!' "No, no, no Laura. No, Laura, NO means NO!' The next day, my mom came into my room at eight in the morning to get me up for school. She said, 'Laura, let's go, you've got to get ready for school. Come on, I'll bring you some juice.' The first words that came out of my mouth were, 'Yeah, but what about the dog?'

-Laura Gross

Some of my greatest successes have been when someone said, *"You can't do that, that's not going to work." "That's impossible! You're this burned up guy in a wheelchair? How could you run for Congress?"* It stimulates me a little bit. I like to prove somebody wrong. The only "NO" that really matters is the one you say to yourself.

-W. Mitchell

The problem is most people are afraid to ask. They're afraid they're going to get a "NO," so they don't. I always say, *"You don't know you're going to get a 'NO' until you ask, and if you don't ask, you've given yourself the 'NO.'* If you want to be confident in confronting a potential 'NO,' ask for a lot of stuff so that you get rejected enough to know you can handle it, and that you didn't die. It's just a numbers game, and somebody's going to say "Yes." If you don't ask, you don't get. If I were talking to me 44 years ago when I was 20, I would say, *"Jack. You need to ask, ask, ask more and not be afraid of rejection whatsoever. You need to rehearse less and take more action."*

-Jack Canfield

I like Go for No! because it's a pattern interrupt, sort of disconnect in someone's mind. Why would we want to go for no? Of course, after you read the book, that you see that not only is "NO" something to not have to fear, not let hold you back, but it's actually something to reframe and embrace. I hear "NO" a lot, and as long as I'm continuing to strive to be somewhere past where I am now, I'll continue to hear NOs. In fact, on an intellectual basis I'll probably start to worry the day I stop hearing NOs, because I'll know that's the day I'm not continuing to progress.

-Bob Burg

My goal was to do three presentations per week, 12 a month, knowing that probably 11 of them would say "No" and my goal was to sign up one person a month for two years. I was going to sign up one person a month for two years, do 12 presentations a month, three a week on my lunches, every single week. Regardless of, it didn't matter what anybody said to me, didn't matter if they were negative or if they were angry or if they were happy or if they were complacent or interested. I was going to do 12 presentations a month for two years, knowing that if I did that, I'd probably sponsor 20 to 30 people. I signed up 19 people in two years. My 19th person signed up a lady in New Mexico who led me to over 12,000 distributors, and over 40,000 customers, and it made me my first million dollars.

-Jordan Adler

I always say that I eat no for breakfast. "No" is the opening dialogue of a conversation. That's all no is. When someone says "No" to you, that's the start of a long negotiation. The way to overcome the word "No" is to make sure you are relentless, no matter what people say to you, you just keep moving forward with tunnel vision and you just attack opportunity with abandon, you seize it. I like to say, you knock it down with a club like a caveman and drag it home. The people who fail the most are the most successful, that's the irony. One "yes" changes your life. So, if you get 100 NOs and one big "YES" every day of your life, you are probably going to be a millionaire.

-Wayne Allyn Root

On an intellectual level, I know that rejection isn't personal, but sometimes I still take it that way because I was this pathologically shy person, and I have worked on that to be able to interact and to be social and to take challenges forward in business. I think what failure does, at its ultimate level, is it shows us who we have to become to get the results we want. Tenacity will always be more important than talent because talent can always be developed. Talent can always be learned. But determination? Perseverance? That's where most people fall down. That's what success is about, it's becoming the person who can do those things.

-Randy Gage

I think the first thing that people have to understand is that everybody fails. I mean everybody. I did a TV show for a number of years in Dallas called "Made for Success," and I interviewed top achievers, the CEO of T-Mobile, the CFO of Microsoft, you name it. Olympic athletes, best-selling authors, every single one of them had a *Go for No!* story—an obstacle, someone telling them they couldn't do it. It's frustrating when you're getting all those NOs but after having all the NOs and now being where I'm at, you really realize that that's where your character was forged, and that's where the lessons were learned, and that's where the wisdom was gained.

-Chris Widener

If you'll just work the system consistently, every single day, you will have so many people in your pipeline to work with that the NOs no longer matter. The problem is most people don't get enough people in the pipeline. So, when the NOs come, it's devastating to them because there's no one else in the pipeline. But those I know who are successful, they have so many people in the pipeline the NOs don't really matter because there's a lot to work with.

-Kody Bateman

It's better to get a real, absolute "No," because then at least you know where you are and you can move on. Nobody has to love cold calling. I kind of think it's fun, but you don't have to love it. You just have to get to neutral because that's a place that you can function. In a selling situation, what's the absolute worst thing that could happen? Well, the worst thing that could happen is you don't get the sale. Again, nobody dies.

-Wendy Weiss

ABOUT RICHARD & ANDREA...

Richard Fenton and Andrea Waltz are the founders Courage Crafters, Inc. and authors of the best-selling book, *Go for No!'*

Speaking on stage together in a unique two-person style of delivery, Richard and Andrea teach people how to reprogram the way they think about the word no to get better results faster while building their courage and confidence. They share specific ways to apply their Go for No! strategy on a daily basis, creating a mindset that encourages tenacity and persistence, especially during tough times.

Before launching their company over 20 years ago, Richard learned to sell at the country's largest fleet dealer from a true master—his father. Andrea originally wanted to work with George Lucas but after getting rejected (she was 8) she went on to build a career in sales and management, meeting Richard at LensCrafters where they decided to launch Courage Crafters. Today, *Go for No"* has become well-known in the world of sales performance training and is widely recognized as the singular best program of its kind.

Their concepts have been featured in hundreds of online and offline publications, including FORBES and SUCCESS MAGAZINE. After hitting #1 on Amazon's Sales & Selling Best Seller list in 2010, their book has remained in the top 50 sales books for the last ten years, earning over 1,000 5-star reviews. Organizations who've benefited from having Richard and Andrea speak to their people include American Express, Mobile Mini, The Pampered Chef (US, Canada & UK), OneHope Wine, Jiffy Lube, Lemongrass Spa, Public Storage, Tervis, American Tire Distributors, Utility Warehouse Ltd., Harry & David, Ameriplan, Lifetouch, and many more.

Richard & Andrea share daily NOtivation on Facebook (www.facebook.com/GoforNo) and on twitter (@GoforNo).

For more information on Go for No!® visit: www.GoforNo.com

For information on having Richard & Andrea speak to your organization, call 800-290-5028, or email them at Info@GoForNo.com.

To watch Richard & Andrea's 15-minute speaking demo, visit www.GoForNoKeynote.com.

THE BOOK THAT STARTED IT ALL!

Sticks and Stones May Break My Bones but "NO" Can Never Hurt Me! That's the lesson twenty-eight-year old copier salesman Eric James Bratton is about to learn. And he's going to learn it from the most unlikely of mentors—himself!

Imagine going to bed one night, then to awaken the next morning in a strange house with no idea of how you got there. Only this house doesn't belong to just anyone—it belongs to you: a wildly successful future version of the person you might one day become, providing you are willing to start doing one simple thing.

And that thing is simple…

To be willing to hear the word "NO" more often.

Before the weekend is over Eric will learn…

- *What it takes to outperform 92% of the world's salespeople*
- *That failing and being a "failure" are two very different things*
- *Why it's important to celebrate success and failure*
- *The five failure levels and how to progress through them*
- *How to get past failures quickly and then move on*
- *That the most empowering word in the world is not yes—it's NO!*
- *And much, much more!*

These lessons are destined to change the way he thinks, the way he sells, and the way he lives forever. And they'll do the same for you!

Available at Amazon.com.

For information on quantity discounts, call 1-800-290-5028 or email us at: Info@GoForNo.com.

No, that's it—this is the end of the workbook.

Now, *go for no!*

Printed in Great Britain
by Amazon

63442888R00052